LOUIS PASTEUR

Troll Associates

LOUIS PASTEUR

by Rae Bains

Illustrated by Dick Smolinski

Troll Associates

Library of Congress Cataloging in Publication Data

Bains, Rae.
    Louis Pasteur.

    Summary: A biography of the nineteenth-century French
scientist who discovered the process for destroying
harmful bacteria with heat and opened the door to the new
science of microbiology.
        1. Pasteur, Louis, 1822-1895.   2. Scientists—France—
Biography—Juvenile literature.   [1. Pasteur, Louis,
1822-1895.   2. Scientists.   3. Microbiology]
I. Smolinski, Dick, ill.   II. Title.
Q143.P2B35   1984   591.2′322′0924 [B] [92]   84-2748
ISBN 0-8167-0148-2 (lib. bdg.)
ISBN 0-8167-0149-0 (pbk.)

For hundreds of years, people had known about the existence of the tiny life forms called microbes. But it took the great nineteenth-century scientist, Louis Pasteur, to recognize the many ways in which microbes affect us. It was Pasteur who showed how to combat some of the deadly diseases caused by microbes. Through his research and discoveries, Pasteur opened the door to a new science known as microbiology.

Louis Pasteur was born in the town of Dôle, France, on December 27, 1822. His father, Jean-Joseph Pasteur, was a tanner, who made beautiful leather from the hides of sheep and cattle. Not long after Louis was born, the family moved to nearby Arbois, a thriving country town on the banks of the Cuisance River.

When Louis was six years old, he started attending a local school. He was a hard-working, serious student, but his teachers did not consider him to be special in any way. In fact, some of them thought he was a slow learner.

While it was true that young Louis did do his lessons slowly, he seldom made a mistake. And his work always looked perfect, with every letter and number carefully and neatly formed.

The Pasteur boy soon showed a talent for drawing. Louis observed things very carefully, gathering all the information he could. Then he set about recreating it on paper. For example, before drawing a butterfly, the boy watched it fly, fold its wings, and take nectar from a flower. When at last he drew it, every detail of the butterfly was perfect.

This talent for careful observation, which began when he was a schoolboy, would become significant later in Pasteur's life. As an adult, Pasteur used his talents for patient study and accurate drawing to reproduce what he observed through a microscope. Even today, scientists can easily identify the yeasts, mold spores, and other microscopic life forms drawn by Pasteur.

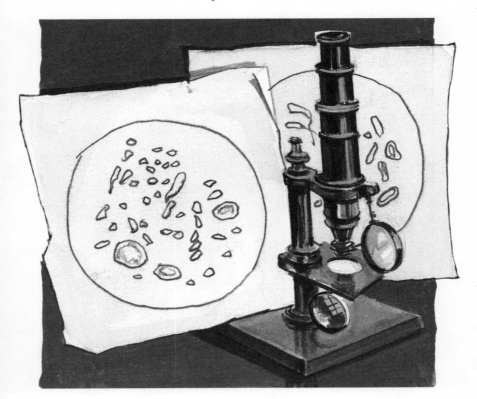

Louis Pasteur entered Arbois High School when he was thirteen. He was still a slow, careful student, but not a slow learner. The young student's grades placed him at the head of his class. In fact, the school principal suggested that the boy think about attending a university. Perhaps, one day, he could even be a teacher. This idea made Louis and his parents very proud.

After two more years at Arbois High School, Louis was enrolled in a fine boarding school in Paris. He was to spend a year there, preparing himself for the difficult college entrance examination.

But Louis did not stay in Paris. He was so homesick that he soon became ill. Mr. Pasteur brought Louis home, and the boy went back to studying at the high school in Arbois.

In 1839, when Louis was seventeen, he felt ready to go away to school. But he still did not feel prepared to take the college examination. So he enrolled at a high school in Besançon, a large town thirty miles away from Arbois.

There, in addition to his regular studies, he took extra science lessons from a chemist. He also continued his painting and acted as assistant teacher of the younger boys. The pay Louis received for teaching helped cover the costs of his schooling. He was a brilliant student at Besançon, graduating with honors in Latin, physics, and mathematics, and receiving a prize for drawing.

Louis took the entrance test for a very excellent teacher's college, called the École Normale, in Paris. He was one of only twenty-two students accepted from all of France.

Yet, because he was fifteenth on the list, he turned down the opportunity to enroll. Instead, Louis spent another year studying. He was determined to do better the next time. He did, placing fourth best in the whole country. And so, in 1843, Louis Pasteur entered college.

While he was studying at the École, Pasteur also took courses at the Sorbonne, the finest university in all of France. At both schools his major interests were chemistry and physics, which he expected to teach.

Pasteur became fascinated by the study of crystals and concentrated on the subject. By the time he received his doctor's degree, in 1847, Pasteur had made the first of his important scientific discoveries. This work, for which he received scholarly recognition, dealt with the structure of crystals.

After graduation, Pasteur was given a teaching post at a high school in a small French city. This seemed such a waste of the young man's talent that a number of prominent chemists arranged for him to be made a university professor. Thus, in 1848, Pasteur became a professor of chemistry at the University of Strasbourg. There, he met Marie Laurent, daughter of a university official. They were married in 1849.

After five happy years at Strasbourg, the Pasteurs moved to Lille. The thirty-two-year-old scientist became professor of chemistry and dean of the faculty of science there. It was at Lille that Pasteur began the work for which he would become world famous.

One day, a man named Bigo came to Pasteur with a problem. His company produced alcohol from beet sugar. The process was called fermentation. Sometimes, the fermentation went well. At other times, something turned the alcohol sour and useless. Bigo asked Pasteur to try to find the cause.

Pasteur studied both the successfully fermented beet sugar and the spoiled sugar under a microscope. He discovered that the spoiled liquid contained millions of rod-shaped cells. The good liquid did not contain these rod-shaped bacteria. Instead, the good liquid was filled with the round yeast cells that caused fermentation. In the spoiled liquid, the rod-shaped bacteria had overrun the round yeast cells. Clearly, the spoilage was caused by the bacteria.

In 1857, following two years of research,
Pasteur presented a report to the Lille
Scientific Society. In it, he described his
work with the beet sugar and offered his
conclusions. But he still had not found a
solution to the problem.

Pasteur continued to search for the
solution. Following his slow, deliberate
method, he found the answer. By heating the

beet sugar to a certain temperature, he destroyed the harmful bacteria.

This process, called pasteurization, was very important to agriculture and industry all over the world. Pasteurization is still the standard method for killing disease-carrying bacteria in milk, cheese, other dairy products, and many different kinds of foods.

Near the end of 1857, the Pasteurs moved to Paris, where Louis assumed the post of director of scientific studies and administrator of the École Normale. He would remain there until he retired in 1888. During those thirty-one years, Pasteur made several scientific breakthroughs.

The first breakthrough was of great significance to France's large silk industry. An epidemic was killing the silkworms that spin the cocoons from which silk is made. Pasteur found that the disease was caused by certain microbes. To eliminate the disease, Pasteur said, the microbe-carriers had to be destroyed. This advice was followed, and the epidemic was ended.

— *Paris 1857*

One of Pasteur's scientific quarrels concerned the way microbes came to be. Many scientists of his time said that microbes simply appeared out of nowhere. This theory was called spontaneous generation. Pasteur believed that living things are produced only by living things. To prove this, he destroyed the microbes in a flask of liquid by heating it. The liquid in the flask remained free of microbes so long as no new microbes were put into it.

Pasteur's interest in controlling microbes led him to the investigation of diseases in animals and humans. He discovered that disease-carrying microbes can be made weaker in a laboratory. These weakened microbes can then be made into a vaccine to prevent disease.

When the vaccine is given to a healthy animal, it causes the animal's body to develop a defense called immunity. Then, if the animal is exposed to the microbe in its strongest form, the animal is safe from the microbe's harmful effects.

Pasteur used the word *vaccination* to describe the process of injecting weakened microbes into animals. His first successful application of this process took place in 1881, when he used it against a terrible

disease called anthrax. Until then, anthrax
killed sheep and cattle by the thousands.
Pasteur's vaccination process was equally
successful in dealing with chicken cholera
and other animal diseases.

In 1882, when Pasteur was sixty years old, he began the study of rabies. Rabies is a disease that is almost always fatal to unprotected animals and people. Within two years he had developed a vaccine that prevented rabies in animals. But Pasteur didn't know if it would work on humans.

Then, in 1885, a boy named Joseph Meister was brought to Pasteur. The boy had been bitten by a dog with rabies and was almost sure to die. Pasteur injected him with the rabies vaccine over a period of weeks. The treatment was a success, and Joseph Meister recovered. Louis Pasteur had once again conquered a dread disease through his scientific genius.

In 1888, Louis Pasteur, weak from a series of strokes, retired from the École Normale. That same year, in his honor, the Pasteur Institute was opened in Paris. It is a center for research into the causes, prevention, and treatment of diseases. Since then, many of the world's great scientists have studied and worked at the Pasteur Institute.

The Institute was a fitting tribute to Louis Pasteur, who died on September 28, 1895. His body was buried on the grounds of the Institute, close to the laboratories he loved so much.